Poems
of
Fact and Fantasy

by

Virginia Artrip Snyder

N. Y. Knott Publishing

©Copyright 1999
by Virginia Artrip Snyder

All rights reserved. No part of this book may be reproduced or transmitted in any form or by any means, electronic or mechanical, including photocopying, recording or by any information storage and retrieval system, without permission in writing from the Publisher.

First Edition

Library of Congress number: 99-095557
ISBN number: 0-9674935-0-1

Printed in the United States of America on recycled paper

N.Y. Knott Publishing
38 South Swinton Avenue
Delray Beach, FL 33444-3654
561-278-5882 / FAX 561-243-2635

10 9 8 7 6 5 4 3 2 1

Virginia and Ross Snyder

*This book is dedicated to Ross,
my husband, lover and best friend,
with loving thanks for forty-five years
of love and support.*

Poems of Fact and Fantasy would not have been possible without the invaluable assistance of three wonderful friends. Lynn Laurenti, Associate Vice President for University Advancement, Florida Atlantic University, edited the manuscript. Jenny Joy, art director, Pass the Word Publications, prepared the manuscript for the printer. Gary Fishman, co-author of *Gator Tales,* a series of children's books, was incredible in the way he handled the logistics, and everything else that needed his special expertise. My sincere thanks for their love and support.

Table of Contents

What is Poetry? 3

Poems of Fact and Fantasy
My Poems 10
Time is Relative 10
Age Difference 11
The News 11
Dream-Borne 12
Comparison 12
Wishing 13
The Heart Divided 13
Gypsy Blood 13
Boy 13
Depression 14
Searching Wind 14
Finale 15
Mistaken Identity 15
Happiness 15
Reminiscences 16
Snow 16
To a Friend 16
Faith 17
Petition 17
My Restless Heart 18
An Evening at Home 19
A Poet's Excuse 19

Gossip	*19*
The Pioneer Life	*20*
Christmas Greeting	*20*
Courage	*21*
A Prayer	*21*
Seeking	*22*
The Great Divide	*22*
Patience	*22*
Lover's Code	*23*
Tribute	*23*
The Sun	*24*
In the Beginning	*24*
Forbidden Journey	*25*
Discourse on Love	*25*
Rainy Day	*26*
Sign of Spring	*26*
Riches	*26*
Metamorphosis	*27*
Open Doors	*27*
Double Loss	*28*
The Veteran	*29*
Revelation	*29*
Beauty and Truth	*30*
The Stoic	*30*
Approach to Life	*31*
The Happy Poet	*31*
Tigers	*32*
Goodbyes	*32*
Loss	*33*
To One Deceived	*33*
A Mother's Viewpoint	*34*
To a Kindred Spirit	*34*
Read with Caution	*34*
The Heart Remembers	*35*
The Funeral	*35*
Indian Summer Romance	*35*

The Factory	*36*
Self-Defense	*36*
It Depends on What You Mean by	*36*
Sumiko Sugawara, a Dear Friend	*37*
Just Another Toy	*37*
I Remember	*38*
Impossible Dream	*38*
Recalling	*38*
Lost at Sea	*38*
Abused Child	*40*
Trust	*40*
The Suicide	*41*
Blind	*41*
Character Sketch	*41*
To My Son	*42*
My Secret	*42*
Autumn	*42*
An Allegory	*43*
It's a Small World	*43*
The Clinic	*43*
A Unitarian Christmas Message	*44*
Enigma	*44*
Sisterhood	*45*
The Quest	*45*
Before We Met	*46*
Unfulfilled	*46*

Poems of Humor

Confused	*47*
To My Doctor	*48*
He Has His Good Points	*49*
His Explanation	*49*
Her Explanation	*49*
Advertisements for Instant Youth	*50*
The Long-Winded Boss	*51*
He's Going to Quit	*51*

Narrow Escape *51*
Alone at Last *51*
Second Time Around *52*
The Philanderer *52*
The Good Sport *52*
He Doesn't Need Directions *52*

Poems for Children
Dolphins *54*
A Kangaroo *54*
A Polar Bear *55*
Elephants *55*
A Pet Raccoon *55*
My Pet Pig *56*
My Pet Skunk, Rose *56*
A Child's Lament *57*
Night Owl *57*
Why? *57*
Young Rebel *57*
Rabbits *58*
Birds and Bees *58*
Little Lamb *59*
The Snake *59*
A Pet Pony *60*
A Duckbill Platypus *60*
The Mink *60*
My Dog *61*
The Goat *61*
My Pet Eel *61*
Acknowledgments *62*
From the Author *66*
Poetry, She Wrote *68*
Photo of Snyder house *70*
Letter from Governor Lawton Chiles *71*
Letter from Representative Suzanne Jacobs *72*

viii

Poems of Fact and Fantasy

What is Poetry?

Poetry is such an intimate experience, whether one is reading or writing it, that any definition of it must necessarily be a personal one.

Many years ago, I was walking along a lane in Virginia, lost in deep, black thoughts, when I became aware of a familiar fragrance in the air. Suddenly I realized it was spring and the first apple blossoms were in bloom.

A moment before, I had been completely oblivious to everything but my own dark mood; I was not even conscious of where I was going, but was following the lane from force of habit. Now, I felt life—vibrant, joyful, all-encompassing, all-pervading life—thrilling through my body. I remember thinking, "This is what it means to be alive, to be one with the universe!"

The memory of that moment, and the effect it had on my life, is still as sharp and clear in my mind as when it happened.

This may seem far afield from the subject of poetry, but actually it is not. When I read poetry, I feel this same exquisite emotion. I am moved by the beauty of the thought, the rhythm of the words, just as I was moved by the smell of apple blossoms that long ago spring. I am moved to joy or sorrow, laughter or tears, because a poet, writing yesterday or a thousand years ago, expressed what was in his or her heart. In words that speak to my heart.

When I first read Edna St. Vincent Millay's *Renascence,* I was in my teens. I recall my amazement when I read the line, "to kiss the fingers of the rain." Why, I knew just what she meant! That was what it felt like when I turned my face up and let the raindrops fall on my eyes and lips.

By the same token, when I read Emily Dickinson's *I Taste a Liquor Never Brewed,* I knew what the poet was really saying. I could see the *two* of us little tipplers leaning against the sun!

Some poetry I find difficult to read aloud because my voice betrays how deeply I am stirred. Kipling *L'envoi* with its majestic scope, Eugene Fields' *Little Boy Blue* with its tender pathos, *The Song of Solomon* with its beauty of expression, *When You are Old* by William Butler Yeats, and Paul Laurence Dunbar's *Compensation* are all such poems.

Poetry has always been a part of my life. Reading it as well as writing it has brought great joy. Poetry has been my friend. It has inspired me, motivated me, consoled me, strengthened me, caused me to laugh and to cry with the poet, and finally, helped me to understand myself.

When I was a child, we had a phonograph record of H. Antoine D'Arcy's poem, *The Face on the Barroom Floor.* I memorized it and used it to tease my sister who would cry each time she heard it.

As the eldest child, it was my responsibility to awaken her each morning to get ready for school. She didn't like to get up, especially in the wintertime when the bedroom was cold. I found that I could get her out of bed by reciting the poem into her ear. I would begin: " 'Twas a balmy summer evening and a goodly crowd was there..." She would cover her head, but I was relentless. When I got to the last lines—"With a fearful shriek, he leaped and fell across the picture—dead"—she was out of bed and chasing me downstairs.

When I was in the fifth grade, I attended a two-room school. Miss Golightly taught fifth, sixth and seventh grades. She was a wonderful teacher. She taught us to love poetry. She read poetry to us and had us memorize certain poems. The last poem she read and had us memorize was *Arcturus in Autumn* by Sara Teasdeale, shortly before school let out for the summer.

Miss Golightly had traveled to Europe and was able to make geography and history come alive. These were two of my favorite subjects. I was eagerly anticipating sixth grade.

To my great disappointment, there was another teacher in her place when school reopened in the fall. When I told my mother, she explained that Miss Golightly was ill, that she had tuberculosis.

She died in October.

At the time of her death, I *knew* why she had chosen the poem about the star that disappears from sight in the fall. She had known.

When in the gold October dusk
I saw you near to setting
...
O, then I knew at last
That my own autumn was upon me,
I felt it in my blood
...

As a teenager, overwhelmed with all the raging passion of first love, I agreed with Ralph Waldo Emerson, "Give all to love, obey thy heart..." (Later loves found me more cautious!)

One of the earliest poets I discovered was Edgar Allen Poe. One poem that made my heart ache, while at the same time thrilling me with its rhythm, its cadence, was *Annabel Lee*.

It was many and many a year ago,
In a kingdom by the sea,
That a maiden there lived whom you may know
By the name of Annabel Lee...

Another was *The Raven*.

Once upon a midnight dreary,
while I pondered weak and weary,
Over many a quaint and curious volume
  of forgotten lore...

Baudelaire described these verses (Poe's) as "That extraordinary elevation, that exquisite delicacy, that accent of immortality which Edgar Allan Poe exacts of the Muse."

When my first love and I broke up, at the age of fifteen, I read *Parting* and realized that Dickinson had described my feelings exactly:

Parting is all we know of heaven
And all we need of hell.

As my social conscience developed, I found myself drawn to poems with a message. When I read *Caliban in the Coal Mines* by Louis Untermeyer, it helped me to understand the coal miners' strikes:

God, we don't like to complain:
We know that the mine is no lark;
But—there's the pools from the rain,
But—there's the cold and the dark.

The Man with the Hoe by Edwin Markham explained the peasants' revolts in Europe:

Bowed by the weight of centuries he leans
Upon his hoe and gazes on the ground,
...
O masters, lords and rulers in all lands,
How will the future reckon with this Man?
...

I do not recall at what point in early life I discovered *Invictus* by William Ernest Henley. I do know that it sustained me during periods of utter despair. When I awoke in a hospital bed at the age of twenty-four after losing a baby and realized that I was blind, (not forever, thank God), the words were there to give me strength:

Out of the night that covers me,
Black as the pit from pole to pole,
I thank whatever gods may be
For my unconquerable soul.
...
I am the master of my fate:
I am the captain of my soul.

With maturity came the realization that Ella Wheeler Wilcox had summed up my philosophy in her poem *The One Need:*

So many laws, so many creeds,
So many ways that wind and wind,
When just the art of being kind
Is all the sad world needs.

The process of creating poetry was described by the tragic German poetess Johanna Ambrosius: "The heart dictates, the mind does the work, and the soul sings the rhythm."

The above conception of how poetry is written could hardly be applied to Karl Jay Shapiro's *The Fly.* I cannot believe that "Oh hideous little bat, the size of snot" was dictated by the heart or sung by the soul! Neither do I think the mind did the work when e.e. cummings wrote, "my father moved through dooms of love through sames of am through haves of give." It sounds like jottings from a psychiatrist's notebook.

These works, and others similar to them, do not awaken any feelings of love or compassion, happiness or sorrow. I feel only disgust and a deep regret that such as this is labeled poetry.

Kahlil Gibran might well have been speaking to the poet as well as the plowman when he wrote, "When you work you are the flute through whose heart the whispering of the hours turns to music." He might also have been speaking of authors of such as *The Fly* when he added, "And if you sing as angels, and love not the singing, you muffle man's ears to the voices of the night."

Poems of Fact and Fantasy

My Poems

There is no room inside my breast
    For all the many things
That I would bury there to rest—
    And so I give them wings.

Time is Relative

Time is not set—
    It does not span
From here to there
    For any man.

It varies much
    From day to day
And who is mortal
    Man to say

That he has fenced—
    On either side—
So much of time,
    So long, so wide?

Age Difference

As long as there is darkness—
    kindly shroud
That takes from us one sense
    of five allowed—
Age has no meaning.
    He who shares my night
Is ageless—until morning
    brings the light.

Second Honorable Mention:
Florida State Poetry Association
Marguerite Evans Memorial Award

The News

The tears came,
Blurring the words
On the paper before me.

But the tears are inside now
Where they are felt but not seen.

I know they are there
Because my thoughts are distorted,
Like images seen through
A rain-drenched pane.

Dream-Borne

My soul has wings
    And soars away
Into far reaches
    Of the day.

My soul has wings
    And in the night
It rides a broomstick
    Out of sight.

Comparison

O, great, majestic tree of oak
What awe in me you do invoke.
You brave the storm, the winter's cold
And grow more proud as you grow old.
Your head is high, your back is straight,
You do not find it hard to wait.
You know what is to be will be;
You do not fear eternity.

We humans do not stand the same;
The mighty oak is not our name.
The weeping willow would be better
For man is evermore a fretter.
We wander here, we wander there,
We bow our heads in deep despair.
We pray what is to be will not
And wait reluctantly our lot.

Wishing

My years to live, perhaps, are few.
Would I could spend them all with you
And know, when Fate puts out the light,
Your lips will kiss my own "Goodnight."

The Heart Divided

The heart, divided, cannot stand
    Its self-inflicted pain.
The suffering it had not planned
    Will make it whole again.

Gypsy Blood

The songs I sang when I was young
    Were light and airy as the breeze,
But now my gypsy songs are sung
    And I am as the quiet trees
That stand serene, because they know
    Their roots are strong and buried deep.
Now when the gypsy breezes blow
    I murmur softly in my sleep.

Boy

Very young and very tender,
    Very shy and very free—
Who can tell, by looking at him,
    What the final man will be?

Depression

Time is a thief
But what have I to lose?
The years go from me,
One way or another,
And life is empty and deserted
As a house from which a family
Has moved out,
That laughed and loved
And warmed its very walls
With joy of living.
No thought of time gone by,
Or present time,
Or time to come,
Intruding.

Searching Wind

What do you seek, O searching wind?
A faithless lover who has sinned?
A broken vow, a long-lost friend?
What does your sad lament portend?

Somewhere, sometime, you will discover
The long-lost friend, the faithless lover,
But never will the gods allow
Safe return of a broken vow.

Finale

And now we are through,
    The race is ended.
The game is over,
    The players winded.

It lasted longer
    Than I had thought.
The prize we won
    Was dearly bought.

Mistaken Identity

When I had never gone astray,
I laughed in such a wicked way
    Men called me wild.
Since I have known your soft embrace
I move at such a dreamy pace,
    They think me mild.

Happiness

When I was young
    I ran to meet
My happiness
    And it was sweet.

Much older now,
    I wait to see
If happiness
    Will come to me.

Reminiscences

When you are old, you'll think of me
    And sigh, "Ah, how I've missed her.
I wonder what my thoughts would be
    If I had ever kissed her?"

When I am old, I'll think of you
    And wonder if you've missed me.
There'd be no wondering at all
    If only you had kissed me.

Snow

White as fleece on a newborn lamb,
    Soft as a baby's breath,
Flakes so gently fluttering down,
    Muffle the sound of death.

Blanket the world in spotless white,
    Cover each unclean stain,
Bringing the quiet peace of night
    Soothing each hurt and pain.

To a Friend

Why should you always walk
    As though you are alone,
When you have friends whose lives
    Touch edges with your own.

Faith

I may recall the twinkle in his eye,
Or how one stubborn lock
    would not lay flat.
Or see the smile that all his frowns belie—
I may remember little things like that.

The memory of his kiss
    may cause me tears,
When I am sad and sitting all alone,
But I'm afraid that, after all these years,
He'd sound just like a
    stranger on the phone.

Petition

Dear Lord, should you not give
    Me happiness, I pray
That you will let me live
    Unhappy in my way.

My Restless Heart

At night, when I have dropped my guard—
    My soul defenseless, half asleep—
I find the acting is too hard
    And so, against my will, I weep.

All day, with heavy lock and chain,
    I keep my restless heart at heel,
But night releases all the pain,
    The aching, longing, that I feel.

And after I am tired and worn,
    My weary heart admits defeat.
It creeps, remorseful, spent and torn,
    To lie, exhausted, at your feet.

Now should you stumble, unaware,
    I beg you to be very kind.
Just pick a spot nearby somewhere
    That won't be difficult to find.

Place my heart there and go your way,
    Lest you, perchance, might trip again,
And, later, by the light of day,
    I'll come and fetch it with my chain.

An Evening at Home

The kitten purrs beside her chair,
    The box is filled with wood.
The light burns low within the room.
    The house is looking good.

The dishes washed and put away,
    The kitchen tidy, neat.
Fresh-cut flowers on the stand,
    A footstool for her feet.

A book of verse is close at hand,
    And robe to snuggle in.
In total loneliness she waits
    For evening to begin.

A Poet's Excuse

I may sound slightly loose
    And even show it.
But I have one excuse—
    I am a poet.

Gossip

In things I do, the gossips find
Much that doth amuse them,
And, so, because I am so kind,
I'll happily confuse them.

The Pioneer Life

A little cabin built of pine,
    Some homemade chairs and table.
I know I'll like this new life fine.
    (That is, if I am able.)

A little brook goes rippling by,
    The birds sing merrily.
One doubt nags at my hopes so high:
    Is this the life for me?

A bear goes romping though the wood,
    The deer are running wild.
This life most certainly is good
    (For husband and for child).

This is that "forest primeval,"
    This, the pioneer life.
One thought alone is worrying me:
    I'm a pioneer wife??

Christmas Greeting

A merry, merry Christmas
    And may your year be bright.
May every day be sunny
    And stars shine every night.

May every wish you whisper
    And every dream come true.
May you be always happy—
    This is my wish for you.

Courage

Since I have held your head
    between my hands
And looked into your eyes
    and breathed your breath,
I find I have the courage
    life demands
And strength to look
    into the face of death.

A Prayer

God, give me strength that I may know
    The peace that all must seek,
Give me the will to bear my cross,
    I know that I am weak.

I need Thy help because, I fear,
    I cannot walk alone.
Give me the courage, if Thou wilt,
    Far more than I have known.

Make me contented with my lot,
    Or make me blind that I
May never see what I should not
    And so, contented, die.

Second Prize, West Virginia State Poetry Contest, sponsored by the State Junior Women's Club

Seeking

I know not what may lie ahead;
    My future may be drear.
My present is but faintly seen
    But still my past is clear.

I know I often saw the light
    But sought the darker way.
What leads my steps toward the night
    When I could have the day?

Why do I roam in shadows dark
    And seek to find, in vain,
A little light, a little spark,
    To warm my heart again?

The Great Divide

I was almost ready to quit
When my personality split,
    But now I just love it,
    There's twice as much of it.
In fact, it has doubled my wit!

Patience

And this is all
    I know, alas.
Though tears may fall,
    They, too, will pass.

Lover's Code

Do you recall
A rainy night?
Raindrops so small,
Like tears, as bright,

In eyes I kissed,
Not needing sight?
God sent the mist
Into our night.

A sign to show
Dreams can come true.
Once, long ago,
Real joy we knew,

Enough to last
Years yet to be.
Our love was cast
Upon life's sea.

Tribute

I dropped a rose upon his grave.
    "What, only one?" you say.
But one rose given by a slave
    Is more than a bouquet.

The Sun

The day is spent, the setting sun,
    With long and rosy fingers,
Lays its caress on everyone
    As lovingly it lingers.

Though loath to leave the world alone,
    Without its loving care,
The light slips quite away from sight
    Before we are aware.

But then the dawn creeps slowly in;
    The black turns soon to gray.
And now the world will smile again.
    It is a lovely day.

In the Beginning

You did not speak of love, it's true,
    But, darling, I was very wise,
For when you looked at me, I knew—
    I saw the longing in your eyes.

But though I turned away and cried,
    "This love cannot be meant for me,"
It mattered not that I denied,
    Your love was there for me to see.

Then when you told your love to me,
    In words your tongue
        found strange and new,
I saw how wonderingly you spoke,
    And, O, dear heart, I clung to you.

Forbidden Journey

My heart is out alone tonight
    And I am waiting here.
It comes in very late, sometimes,
    But finds me always near.

I often wish that I could go
    On some wild journey, too.
But I dare not, because, I know
    I would fly straight to you.

So what use, then, for me to roam,
    To knock upon your gate,
For you would only send me home.
    And so I sit and wait.

Discourse on Love

Now in the moon's bright light,
Now in the still of night,
Now you are not in sight,
    Let me recall.

That the moon was as bright in times past,
That the full of the moon does not last,
That the fullness of love goes as fast,
    Beyond recall.

Rainy Day

A day like this
Was meant to be
A foretaste of
Eternity.

With dripping skies
And clouds of gray,
On dragging feet
It goes its way.

Sign of Spring

I saw a robin and my heart,
    Which had 'til then been sad,
Was cheered a little and I knew
    Someday I would be glad.

Somehow, it seems a touch of spring
    Has centered in my soul.
Someday, my world of shattered dreams
    Will once again be whole.

Riches

Count not your wealth in silver
    Nor reckon it in gold,
Or else you may discover,
    When you are bent and old,
Riches are not made of things
    That can be bought and sold.

Metamorphosis

There was a time, not long ago,
    When I could look at you,
And say, "What does that so-and-so
    Think I am going to do?

Why, I could hold him in my arms,
    From setting sun 'til dawn,
And though I might admire his charms,
    All I would do is yawn."

Then I was frigid, just like ice,
    Unmoved by mad desire.
I'd like to ask you, was it nice
    To make me out the liar?

Open Doors

Do not shut fast the door
As you pass swiftly through,
But open it the more
For those who follow you.

Do not replace the bar
For someday you may learn
To leave each door ajar—
You may, yourself, return.

Honorable Mention,
Franklin P. Davis (national) poetry contest

Double Loss

He was the first—
    The one who knew
Her greatest love—
    And she was true.

When he had gone,
    She looked in vain
For such a love
    To come again.

Each time she thought
    It was the same,
But lower still
    Burned passion's flame.

The years passed by
    And she grew old,
Amazed to find
    Her heart so cold.

Second Honorable Mention,
Florida State Poets Association,
Anita Fairbanks Memorial Award

The Veteran

His eyes are empty and his mind
    Dulled with too much seeing.
Though he has not by choice gone blind,
    He is tired of being.

His eyes were made to look on sights
    God never meant to be.
Small wonder that his days are nights,
    Each one eternity.

And he will never be the same.
    We must accept this truth.
Though we speak lovingly his name,
    We do not know this youth.

Revelation

I touched your hand.
    How could I know
My heart would want
    Your nearness so,
Or feel, when you
    Were close to me,
That I had known
    Infinity?

Beauty and Truth

I lived for Beauty
    And not for Truth,
But that was in
    My foolish youth.

As I grew older
    And knew my duty,
I lived for Truth,
    And not for Beauty.

Now that my life
    Is almost done,
I know that Beauty
    And Truth are one.

Honorable Mention, Florida State Poetry Contest, sponsored by the Daytona Beach Chapter of the National League for American Penwomen

The Stoic

Life beats against me as I go,
But I embrace Life, murmuring low,
"Come, Lover, welcome—we are one.
Why should we fight and spoil the fun?"

Approach to Life

I say yes to life
But not until I'm sure.
Then I get on with it;
I don't look back.

I have always said yes to life
But my answer comes quicker now.

In the dim past, I needed years
To say yes to living.
Now I need only moments
To say yes to loving.

At the same time,
I have learned to wait,
For waiting means anticipation
Rather than frustration.

And, for good or ill,
I am struck by the humor of life.

The Happy Poet

I want to write a poem
    Because I searched so long
For one whose very presence
    Could fill my heart with song.

But now that I have found him,
    Apart from all the crowd,
I cannot write my poem
    For singing it aloud.

Tigers

My aunt loved butterflies.
She would watch them play
Outside her window
And marvel at their delicate beauty.

My aunt hated corruption
And violence.
A report of police brutality
Would make her furious.

She would call officials,
Write letters to the editor,
Even picket.
But she loved butterflies,
Especially tiger butterflies.

Goodbyes

Goodbyes are always sudden,
    As everybody knows.
We never really hear them
    Until the whistle blows.

Blue Ribbon Award,
Southern Poetry Association

Third Prize,
Ohio Poetry Day Contest

Loss

Three little mounds all in a row
    Are all that I can see,
Yet, underneath each stone, I know,
    There is a part of me.

A very, very tender part
    That will not live again.
Each one was carried near my heart
    And borne with greatest pain.

Then, when the miracle of birth
    Had given them to me,
God bore them, with relentless mirth,
    Off to eternity.

To One Deceived

Some woman lied to you
    And you believed.
That woman was a fool
    To treat you so.
Do not feel bitter
    That you were deceived—
Be glad you are among
    The ones who know!

A Mother's Viewpoint

My daughter's husband is so good,
    He loves to fetch and carry.
He treats her like she is a queen.
    Now that's the kind to marry!

But Junior did not have such luck,
    He was a fool to wed.
The poor boy eats his breakfast out
    While she stays home in bed!

To a Kindred Spirit

If sometimes in your laugh I hear
    A note that is not true
I'll not betray your act, my dear,
    For I've been bluffing, too.

Read with Caution

Take not too seriously
    my verse;
Think not that all
    I say is true.
My poems, I fear,
    would sound much worse
Had I not told a fib or two.

The Heart Remembers

Gentle touching,
Flesh against soft flesh,
Leaves no imprint—
But the heart remembers.

The Funeral

The air is heavy with
    the feel of fear.
The hot oppressiveness
    when death is near
Has closed upon their throats
    with sinuous grasp
And chokes their breath
    as they approach the bier.

Indian Summer Romance

Unexpected warmth,
after the first shocking chill
of Autumn's cold breath.

The Factory

Outside, the grass
    is green, the sun
Shines down alike
    on everyone.
Inside, the bright
    fluorescent glow
Shines down alike
    on all below.

Self-Defense

The cop saw the teenager
    turn and run.
Too bad for the boy;
    the cop had a gun.
"I thought he was armed,"
    the officer said.
The boy said nothing
    because he was dead.

It Depends on What You Mean by…

I'll love you forever
He cooed in her ear.
Too bad, his "forever"
Was only a year.

Sumiko Sugawara, a Dear Friend

The waves
Came rushing in
Over my open hand,
Then gently took my love away
To rest.

*Written for Sumiko's husband, Mitsuo,
who brought some of her ashes from Japan
to the waves off Delray Beach, which she
loved so much.*

Just Another Toy

Daddy, please buy me a gun.
All the other kids have one.
I could really have some fun.
I won't shoot at anyone.

I could carry it to school.
Much more fun than playing pool.
It would be so very cool
Just like buying a new tool.

Here's an Uzi for you, son.
Just don't shoot at anyone.

I Remember

There were not many good times
    In life when I was small.
Since there are so very few,
    They're easy to recall.

Memories are as sharp and clear
    As anything could be.
Close my eyes and they are there,
    So much a part of me.

Dewdrops dripping from a leaf,
    Small pebbles in a stream,
Deep, dark woods in which to hide,
    A secret place to dream.

To find a four-leaf clover
    Was always such a thrill.
To catch a little minnow,
    To climb a little hill.

But then there were the beatings—
    I think of them as well.
Although there were some good times,
    My early years were hell.

Impossible Dream

Before me lies the castle
But I cannot cross the moat.
The drawbridge is not lowered
And I do not have a boat.

Recalling

Do not despair if sometimes
One you have loved very much
Yearns for another's kisses,
Or thrills at another's touch.
Unless your heart is broken,
Can you not forgive, forget,
And let all pain lie buried?
Recalling will hurt you yet.
Eyes that have known weeping
Fall fast asleep, by and by.
One must be always keeping
Restraint on eyes that would cry.
    Must I always let you go,
    Even when I want you so?

Lost at Sea

He rests within the cool, green deep,
    Rocked gently to and fro.
It seems a peaceful way to sleep
    If one is forced to go.

A grave on shore is hard and dark,
    And narrow as can be.
It's better on an ocean couch
    To wait eternity.

Abused Child

Feelings.
What are they?
To feel.
What is that?
To cry.
Who cries?
To love.
Love?
I've heard of that.
But what is love?
Warmth,
Affection,
Softness,
Gentleness—
All of these
Are foreign to me.

I am tough.
I am indifferent.
I am alone.
I am lonely.
I cannot feel.
I cannot love.

Trust

Because
My heart is true,
You should not think it strange
That, when I see somebody new,
I smile.

The Suicide

To those who come and question, "Why?"
    This answer you may give:
The reason that she chose to die:
    It was too hard to live.

Blind

"Wake up," I told myself.
    "Just try once more.
You are awake now,
    can't you see the light?
It must be day,
    for all the sounds around
Are different from
    the silences of night."

"So you're awake now. Good.
    Then here's your tray."
Somewhere in the blackness,
    soft and kind.
It was my nurse, *the one
who came by day.*
And then I realized
    that I was blind.

Character Sketch

Profound, intense—
Lacks common sense.

To My Son

Happiness
Is a feeling
That swells inside,
Until the pressure
Forces tears
From the eyes.

My Secret

He's dying, they say, and look at me
    With eager eyes, to know my pain.
But they are not aware, you see—
    To me, he cannot die again.

Autumn

I'll meet you there.
Remember where
We used to meet before?

The trees are bare
But I don't care—
I'll meet you there once more.

The birds that sing
Will come with spring
And we will not be here.

But do not cry
For you and I
Have had our spring, my dear.

An Allegory

I stumbled and I hurt my toe.
Someone as old as I should know
To be more wary, walk with care,
For stones are scattered everywhere.
I cannot tell (although I try)
About the hurting, while I cry.

Its a Small World

It's true
The world is small
And getting smaller still,
And how the end will come, who knows,
Or cares.

The Clinic

Shuffling feet, uneasy glances,
    Nervous coughs and throats gone dry.
Eyes that meet but never linger,
    Empty phrases, baby's cry.

Cold unfriendly, white walls gleaming—
    Here no warmth, no tender touch.
Who has time for friendly gestures?
    Who, in fact, would care that much?

A Unitarian Christmas Message

Merry Christmas to the Christians,
Merry Christmas to the Jews,
Christians Scientists and Quakers—
And Unitarians, if they choose.

Happy Birthday, Baby Jesus,
And, although the thought be new,
Happy Birthday, little heathen—
And little Unitarian, too.

Let us all rejoice, be merry,
Let us all give forth with song.
Do you feel a little scary?
Think the Christians could be wrong?

Just in case, we'll take no chance.
After all, it might be true—
So we'll worship like the Christians,
Jews and Unitarians do.

Also, lest they be forgotten,
Happy Birthday, dear Vishnu,
Confucius, Buddha and Mohammed—
And William Ellery Channing, too.

Enigma

So I take things too seriously?
    Of course I do.
But then sometimes, mysteriously,
    I'm laughing too.

Sisterhood

Take thou thy sister's burden
    Upon thy back instead.
Her shoulders may be weary,
    The thorns may pierce her head.

The cross that she is bearing
    May be a heavy load.
The thorn-crown she is wearing
    Leave blood drops on the road.

Though your heart may be aching
    And you have cause to cry,
Your sister's heart is breaking
    Can you, then, pass her by.

The Quest

True happiness is hard to find,
    The perfect moment rare,
And only those who are not blind
    Look for it everywhere.

They know there is no certain site,
    No special day or year.
We must expect it, else we might
    Disguise it with a tear.

Then when the gods at last relent
    And let us see the stars,
We find how much of love was spent
    In beating at the bars.

Before We Met

When you cried before we met,
    Who kissed your tears away?
When you laughed, do you forget
    Who joined in the play?

Dreams you fashioned in your youth,
    Sharing with another,
Darling, please tell me the truth,
    Say it was your mother.

Unfulfilled

The song unsung,
Notes waiting in my heart,
How can I share its joy
If I am mute?

The song half-sung,
Imprisoned in my throat,
How can it gain release
While I'm enslaved?

The cup half-drained,
So lovingly caressed,
How can I turn away
While thirst consumes me?

Poems of Humor

Confused

If I should rant and rave
Would you please set me straight?
I'd rather rave than rant,
Unless it is too late.

When day has turned to night
And night has turned to day,
I worry, is it right?
Should it work out that way?

The seasons come and go,
Or do they go and come?
I'd really like to know.
It makes me feel so dumb.

All night I toss and turn,
Or do I turn and toss?
I'd really like to learn.
I feel so at a loss.

To My Doctor

The waiting room is jammed and packed
With joints that ache and bones all cracked.
With "Pains right *here,* and right *there,* too."
"What do *you* think I ought to do?"
"All night I never sleep a wink."
"It's enough to drive a man to drink."
"He's cried 'til I'm worn to a *string.*"
"Indeed, he won't eat *anything.*"
"I wish you'd give my *heart* a check."
"Honestly, I'm a *nervous wreck.*"
Doctor, how can you stand the pace
And still maintain a smiling face?
When you look out and see us there,
Do you not scream and tear your hair?
Now I'm not like the *rest,* you see.
I've a split personality.
Sometimes one of me is ailing,
Then, again, the *other's* failing.
Sometimes *complexes* cause the trouble,
Other times, I just see *double.*
Must be *something,* to tell the truth,
That happened to me in my *youth.*
At *three a.m.* I'm apt to rise
And write a sonnet to his *eyes!*
At *six,* there's no arousing me.
Doctor what *can* the matter be?

(continued on page 49)

(continued from page 48)

When noontime finds the beds unmade
And me still lounging in the shade,
I am not *really* neglecting duty,
I've just composed an *Ode to Beauty.*
My hear is bound, my soul is free,
But there *is something* wrong with me!

He Has His Good Points

It's true he isn't very smart
And doesn't have much hair,
But his father made a fortune
In ladies' underwear.

His Explanation

I'm just a homebody at heart,
I really do not like to roam.
To speak of it tears me apart,
But I'm misunderstood at home.

Her Explanation

It's not that I'm so very good,
But I do like discretion.
I don't want everyone to know
I'm headed for damnation.

Advertisements for Instant Youth

Eat all you want and lose weight.
In weeks, we'll make you look great.
    Lose bulging hips,
     Get pouty lips
And be somebody's playmate.

Do you want smooth, slimmer thighs?
Get rid of your baggy eyes?
    You're ugly now,
    Look like a cow.
Let's face it, you are no prize.

Cheer up. We'll make you look right.
We'll banish the cellulite,
    Unhook your nose,
    Straighten your toes,
Pull your face muscles up tight.

Tumescent liposuction
Sounds like sexual seduction.
    Augmentation,
    Implantation,
And even breast reduction.

Let the doctor take over
If you want a makeover.
    But don't blame me
    If what you see
Is black and blue all over!

The Long-Winded Boss

The meeting was quite a disaster.
It should have concluded much faster,
    But the boss' bad jokes
    Kept boring the folks—
He sure missed his calling as pastor.

He's Going to Quit

Smoking has no earthly use.
Habit is his sole excuse.

He will never smoke again;
He is going to break the chain

That enslaves him, link by link.
From now on, he plans to drink.

Narrow Escape

All I have left is our photograph
    With me in my bridal gown.
I sit and look at your face and laugh—
    I'm glad I got out of town!

Alone at Last

You're gone and I am all alone.
It makes me want to howl.
    I miss such things
    As bathtub rings
And lipstick on the towel.

Second Time Around

When the widow met the old geezer,
He did all that he could to please her,
    But she kept saying, "No,
    You'll just have to go—"
Until he filled up her deep freezer.

Honorable Mention
Ohio Poetry Day Contest

The Philanderer

He never meant to deceive her,
He was just an overachiever.
    But she called his bluff
    When she'd had enough—
And did it with a meat cleaver.

The Good Sport

He was always such a good sport.
He'd stop at the bar for a snort
    While she cooked the meal
    And watched for the heel—
She finally saw him in court.

He Doesn't Need Directions

Of course, I know where I'm going.
    Why did you ask me that?
I know exactly where I'm going.
    I just don't know where I'm at.

*These poems for children are dedicated
to my nine-year-old grandniece,
Nicole Campbell, a budding poet.*

Monsters

Monster, monster, under my bed.
Monster, monster, in my head.
Monster, monster everywhere.
Monster, monster, *are you there?*

Nicole Campbell

Poems for Children

Dolphins

I went to Sea World with my Dad
And saw the dolphins in a pool.
"Now, there's a pet I wish I had.
It would be so very cool."

When I said that, Dad looked at me
And then he slowly shook his head.
"Dolphins are happy when they're free.
They're just like us that way," he said.

A Kangaroo

One day when we went to the zoo,
My Dad showed me a kangaroo.

Her front legs were so very small
It seemed she had no legs at all.

But her hind legs were big and strong,
I saw, as she hop-hopped along.

"Her baby's not on mama's back—
Just look! He's tucked in her *front* pack!"

A Polar Bear

A polar bear loves snow and ice,
But though I asked my Daddy twice
If I could have one for a pet,
He told me, "Honey, you're all wet!
Our weather is too hot for him
And there's no place for him to swim
Where chunks of ice go floating by—
But here's a teddy bear, don't cry."

Elephants

The elephants are very big.
They weigh a lot more than a pig.
I couldn't keep one in a pen
The way I could a little hen.
Although it surely would be fun,
I will not ask my Dad for one.

A Pet Raccoon

I had a raccoon I fed with a spoon.
    It liked to sleep on my lap.
Then I heard big brother say to Mother,
    "It sure would make a neat cap!"

My Pet Pig

One time, I had a little pig.
He really wasn't very big,
But he could make a lot of noise
When playing with the girls and boys.

One day, he squealed so very loud
That suddenly there was a crowd
Of people who had heard his cry
And thought he was about to die.

But when they saw it was in play,
Then everybody went away.
My little pig just raised his snout
And said, "What was *that* all about?"

My Pet Skunk, Rose

Sweet little Rose, black and white.
Keeps me awake every night.
I'm afraid she's going to spray
And the smell won't go away.
Then what will my Mama say?
It will be a real bad day.

Mama said, "You'll be surprised.
I had your skunk deodorized."

A Child's Lament

My life, it seems
Is made up just
Of things I *like*
And things I *must*.

Night Owl

At night when others "hit the hay,"
I want to stay awake and play.
At dawning when they all arise,
I cannot open up my eyes.

Why?

When she sees soldiers made of lead
My Mama smiles and nods her head.
But when my little drum appears,
Why does she cover up her ears?

Young Rebel

When I would walk in the moonlight
    They say, "It is cold, you will freeze."
But I *like* to walk in the moonlight
    And so I will do as I please.

Rabbits

I asked my Mommy why the rabbits
    Don't run instead of hop.
She said it's just one of those habits
    That's very hard to stop.

Birds and Bees

I'd like to know
    How birds and bees
Can stay outside
    And never freeze.

Yet when the wind
    Is cold and blows,
Or if it rains
    A bit or snows,

My Mom makes me
    Put on my coat
And ties a scarf
    Around my throat.

But when I ask
    My Mama, "Why?"
She says I must
    'Cause I can't fly!'

Little Lamb

I'd like to be
    A little calf
But if I were,
    I could not laugh.

I'd also like
    To be a bird
But then I could
    Not say a word.

I can't be all
    The things I wish—
A bumblebee
    Or flying fish—

So I will be
    Just what I am,
'Cause Mom says I'm
    Her *Little Lamb!*

The Snake

Some people keep snakes in their house.
For dinner, they feed them a mouse.
If snakes would eat grass or a nut,
Or if they would keep their mouth shut
And not eat anything at all—
Just lie around their cage or crawl—
But, come to think of it, they'd die
And I am sure that I would cry.
So I won't ask my Mom for one.
Now all the mice can have some fun.

A Pet Pony

I rode a pony at the park.
    It was a lot of fun.
When I got off, I asked my Mom,
    "Would you please buy me one?"

"It's just a tiny horse," I pled,
    "And it will not grow up."
My Mom replied, "That's what you said
    When I gave you a pup."

A Duckbill Platypus

The duckbill platypus lives far away
    In a land called "Down Under."
Where in the world did it get such a name?
    It really makes me wonder.

I know what a duck looks like, with its bill.
    I know it can swim and quack.
But the duckbill platypus puzzles me.
    Are there feathers on its back?

The Mink

One day, I saw a little mink.
He looked at me and gave a wink.
"I'm on my way to catch a boat
Before they put me in a coat.
I'm not as dumb as they may think,
Just because I am a mink."

My Dog

My little dog
    Is very smart
And lots of tricks
    He knows by heart.
But even though
    I try and try,
I can't teach him
    To wink *one* eye.

The Goat

Little goats love to eat grass.
You have to be careful, alas.
    They like to attack
    When you turn your back—
For a pet? I think I will pass.

My Pet Eel

I once had an eel for a pet.
I still feel the slippery thing yet.
    He would wiggle and squirm
    Like an oversized worm—
It's something I just can't forget.

Acknowledgments

What is Poetry?	*The Candlelight Poetry Journal*, Spring 1997

Poems of Fact and Fantasy

My Poems	*Echoes of West Virginia* *Palmetto Voices* *The Candlelight Poetry Journal*
Time is Relative	*The Candlelight Poetry Review*
The News	*Muse*, an anthology *Piedmont Literary Review*
Dream-Borne	*Jefferson Republican* Orlando Sentinel-Star's *Galley Proof* *Echoes of West Virginia* *The Lyric*
Comparison	*Jefferson Republican* *Highlander*
Wishing	*Highlander*
The Heart Divided	*Echoes of West Virginia* *Highlander*
Gypsy Blood	*The Lyric* *The Candlelight Poetry Journal*
Boy	*The Pen*
Depression	*Piedmont Literary Review*

Searching Wind	*The Beacon of Life*, an anthology, Armadillo Poetry Press
Finale	*Jefferson Republican* *Echoes of West Virginia*
Mistaken Identity	Orlando Sentinel-Star's *Galley Proof* *Denial is not a River in Egypt*, an anthology, Creativity Unlimited Press
Happiness	Southern Poetry Association
Reminiscences	Orlando Sentinel-Star's *Galley Proof* *Reflections*
Snow	*Jefferson Republican* *Nashville Newsletter*
To a Friend	*Evening Post*, Charleston, SC *Poet's Reed* *Hearth & Home*, anthology, Armadillo Poetry Press
My Soul Has Wings	Orlando Sentinel-Star's *Galley Proof*
Half-Forgotten Love	*The Beacon of Life*, anthology, Armadillo Poetry Press
Petition	Orlando Sentinel-Star's *Galley Proof*
My Restless Heart	*The Neovictorian/Cochlea*
An Evening at Home	*Hearth & Home*, anthology, Armadillo Poetry Press
A Poet's Excuse	Orlando Sentinel-Star's *Galley Proof*
Gossip	*Echoes of West Virginia* Orlando Sentinel-Star's *Galley Proof* *Highlander*
The Pioneer Life	*Jefferson Republican*
Christmas Greeting	*Highlander* *The Candlelight Poetry Journal*

Courage	*Hearth Songs Journal* *The Poetry Hour*
A Prayer	*Jefferson Republican* *Echoes of West Virginia*
Seeking	*Jefferson Republican*
The Great Divide	*The Spark of Laughter*, anthology, Armadillo Poetry Press
Patience	*Hearth Songs Journal*
Lover's Code	*Embers*, anthology, Armadillo Poetry Press
Tribute	*Hearth Songs Journal*
The Sun	*Jefferson Republican*
In the Beginning	*Fire & Ice*, anthology, Armadillo Poetry Press
Forbidden Journey	*Poet's Reed*
Discourse on Love	*Echoes of West Virginia*
Rainy Day	*Jefferson Republican* *Echoes of West Virginia* Orlando Sentinel-Star's *Galley Proof* *Raintown Review*
Sign of Spring	*The Pen*
Riches	*Yesterday's Magazette*
Metamorphosis	*Fire & Ice*, anthology, Armadillo Poetry Press
Open Doors	*Evening Post*, Charleston SC *American Courier* Orlando Sentinel-Star's *Galley Proof* *Echoes of West Virginia* *Fiesta*
Double Loss	*The Candlelight Poetry Review*
The Veteran	*The Lyric*

Revelation	*Echoes of West Virginia* Orlando Sentinel-Star's *Galley Proof* *Highlander* *The Pen*
The Stoic	*Senior Life & Boomer Times*
Approach to Life	*The Candlelight Poetry Journal*
The Happy Poet	*Echoes of West Virginia* *The Candlelight Poetry Journal*
Tigers	*The Candlelight Poetry Journal*
Goodbyes	*The Poetry Hour*

Poems of Humor

Confused	*Palm Peach Post*
Narrow Escape	*The Spark of Laughter*, anthology, Armadillo Poetry Press
He Doesn't Need Directions	*Idaho News Observer*

Poems for Children

A Child's Lament	Orlando Sentinel-Star's *Galley Proof* *Highlander*
Night Owl	*Highlander*
Why?	*The Playground*, anthology, Armadillo Poetry Press
Young Rebel	*Highlander*
Rabbits	*The Playground*, anthology, Armadillo Poetry Press
Birds and Bees	*The Playground*, anthology, Armadillo Poetry Press
Little Lamb	*Echoes of West Virginia*

From the Author

I have written poetry since I was a child, but I was in my 20's before I had an opportunity to learn if my poems were any good. I was working on a weekly newspaper and the editor was publishing a poem each week on the editorial page. I began slipping my poems on his desk, signed "N.Y. Knott," and he published each one.

When he began worrying about possible plagiarism, I confessed. From then on, he published them over my real name. Encouraged by this, and a 1949 column comparing my writing favorably to that of Emily Dickinson and Edna St. Vincent Millay, I began submitting poems to poetry journals and other publications. Many were published and I received several awards.

After Ross and I married in 1954, I still wrote poetry, but was usually too busy to do anything with it. When I turned 75, I reactivated my poetry-writing career. Since that time, I have had many poems accepted for publication in poetry journals and anthologies.

I have been reading my poetry on the *American Senior Side* radio show (WXEL 90.7 FM, PBS affiliate, Boynton Beach, Florida) hosted by Chuck Zink. At the urging of Chuck and other friends and relatives, I decided to publish this selection, written over a 60-year period.

I have purposely not arranged the poems in chronological order or in categories. This will allow the reader to guess when they were written and which are autobiographical.

Virginia Artrip Snyder

Poetry, She Wrote

Virginia Artrip Snyder is a true Renaissance woman. Born on a farm near Winchester, Virginia, November 27, 1920, she was a late-blooming college student who received a degree in government and politics from Florida Atlantic University when she was 45. She went on to become a newspaper reporter for the Fort Lauderdale News and the Boca Raton News, receiving seven national, state and local awards for investigative reporting in 1974, the last year she was a reporter.

A highly effective community activist, she spearheaded the establishment of many public service agencies in South Palm Beach County while working as a reporter and later during 22 years as a nationally known private investigator.

During her career as a private investigator, she crusaded tirelessly against injustice, often donating her services to those she felt had been unfairly convicted of crimes. Thanks in part to her dedicated efforts, six men on Florida's death row were saved from execution. A real-life version of Agatha Christie's famous "Miss Marple," Virginia used her wits as her main weapon with results so spectacular that she became the inspiration for *Murder, She Wrote.*

Her many awards include being named one of fourteen "Outstanding Women of Florida" in 1975 by then-Governor Reubin Askew, and one of "Florida's Finest" in 1996 by Governor Lawton Chiles.

Since early childhood, Virginia has loved both reading and writing poetry. After closing her investigative agency on December 31, 1998, she decided to devote herself full-time to writing. This is her first published volume of verse. She also has written two nonfiction manuscripts on her life and work and has two more in progress.

Virginia and her husband, Ross, live in Delray Beach, Florida. Their historical home, pictured on the following page, dates back to 1902.

Contributed by Lynn Laurenti,
Associate Vice President for University Advancement,
Florida Atlantic University

Lynn Laurenti has known Virginia for 35 years.

Virginia and Ross have lived in the oldest residential house in Delray Beach, Florida, in the Old School Square Historic District, since 1971. Not pictured are the lush gardens with the many tropical fruit trees and ornamentals surrounding the house and adding to its charm. "A great place for a poet to live."

STATE OF FLORIDA
Office of the Governor
THE CAPITOL
TALLAHASSEE, FLORIDA 32399-0001

LAWTON CHILES
GOVERNOR

April 28, 1997

Ms. Virginia Artrip Snyder
Virginia Snyder, Inc.
38 South Swinton Avenue
Delray Beach, FL 33444-3654

Dear Virginia:

Thanks so much for sending *What is Poetry*? I have always had a great appreciation of poetry and great admiration for those talented individuals who are willing to share with the world those deep emotions through which poetry flows.

I was touched by your remembrance of the effect on your life of the scent of apple blossoms. Being a man of nature myself, I agree that nothing so moves a person as the beauty of nature and the feeling of being one with the universe.

I appreciate your sharing some of your thoughts and a moving sample of your poetry. You have given the world a gift that transcends time. Your works will no doubt be studied and enjoyed by generations of school children and their parents. You are truly one of "Florida's Finest."

With warm personal regards, I am

Sincerely,

LAWTON CHILES

LC/pm

Florida House of Representatives
Suzanne Jacobs
Representative, District 88

990 S. Congress Ave., Suite 5
Delray Beach, FL 33445
561-274-4690 (Delray)
561-433-3666 (WPB)

Suite 212, The Capitol
402 S. Monroe St.
Tallahassee, FL 32399-1300
850-488-1662

July 8, 1999

The Florida Commission on the Status of Women
Attn: Women's Hall of Fame
Office of the Attorney General
The Capitol
Tallahassee, FL 32399-1050

Dear Ms. Weatherford:

It is my distinct honor to nominate Virginia Artrip Snyder to the Florida Women's Hall of Fame. During the fifteen years that I have known Ms. Snyder, my appreciation of her contributions has grown from sincere to awestruck. As the state's second female private investigator, award-winning journalist, published poet, founder of the Mae Volen Senior Center and Florence Fuller Day Care Center, she has improved the quality of life, and in six specific cases has saved the lives, of Floridians.

This remarkable woman's contributions - to our community, to the state and, via the media, to the millions of people who are aware of her work - merit ongoing recognition. Virginia is a vibrant example of how much a woman can accomplish. Her intellect, bravery and persistence qualify her as a hero.

Surely Virginia Snyder would be an asset to the Florida Women's Hall of Fame. And surely Floridians will benefit from the continued recognition of her unique contributions to a civil society. Highlights of Virginia's accomplishments are presented in an attachment to this letter. Thank you and the Women's Hall of Fame Committee for your thoughtful consideration to my nominee, Virginia Snyder.

Sincerely,

Suzanne Jacobs
State Representative
District 88

SJ:RC:RC

Committees: Vice Chair, Government Rules and Regulations • Elder Affairs and Long Term Care • Finance and Taxation
Real Property and Probate • Public Responsibility Council